ENGLISH IN ACTION

THIRD EDITION

Workbook **2**

ENGLISH IN ACTION

THIRD EDITION

BARBARA H. FOLEY

ELIZABETH R. NEBLETT

Australia · Brazil · Mexico · Singapore · United Kingdom · United States

National Geographic Learning,
a Cengage Company

English in Action Level 2 Workbook
Third Edition
Barbara H. Foley and Elizabeth R. Neblett

Publisher: Sherrise Roehr

Executive Editor: Sarah Kenney

Managing Development Editor:
   Claudienma Mimó

Senior Development Editor: Lewis Thompson

Associate Development Editor: Katie Davis

Assistant Editor: Becky Long

Media Researcher: Leila Hishmeh

Director of Global Marketing: Ian Martin

Product Marketing Manager: Dalia Bravo

Sr. Director, ELT & World Languages:
   Michael Burggren

Production Manager: Daisy Sosa

Content Project Manager: Beth Houston

Manufacturing Customer Account Manager:
   Mary Beth Hennebury

Composition: Lumina Datamatics, Inc.

Cover/Text Design: Lisa Trager

Art Director: Brenda Carmichael

Cover Image: © Anand Radhakrishnan

For permission to use material from this text or product, submit all requests online at **cengage.com/permissions**
Further permissions questions can be emailed to
permissionrequest@cengage.com

English in Action 2 Workbook
ISBN: 978-1-337-90599-2

National Geographic Learning
20 Channel Center Street
Boston, MA 02210
USA

Locate your local office at **international.cengage.com/region**

Visit National Geographic Learning online at **NGL.Cengage.com/ELT**
Visit our corporate website at **www.cengage.com**

Printed at CLDPC, USA, 01-23

CONTENTS

Welcome 2

1 My School 8

2 The Family 14

3 Home 20

4 A Typical Day 26

5 Airport Jobs 32

6 Safety at Work 38

7 Eating Out 44

8 Good Weekend / Bad Weekend 50

9 Last Weekend 56

10 Growing Up 62

11 People and Places 68

12 Goals and Plans 74

13 Vacations 80

Spelling Rules and Irregular Verb List 86

Credits 88

WELCOME

A Complete with a pronoun from the box.

She	Her	He	His	They	Their

1.

_____Her_____ name is Bibiana. _____ is from Slovakia. _____ is twenty-seven years old. _____ is single. _____ is a student.

2.

_____ name is Shen. _____ is from China. _____ native language is Mandarin. _____ is single. _____ is a student. _____ works in the university science lab.

3.

_____ names are Akila and Nasrin. _____ are college students. _____ are from Qatar. _____ native language is Arabic. _____ are classmates.

B Write each sentence again. Use pronouns for the underlined words.

1. The students are busy.

   They are busy.

2. The classroom is large.

   _____

3. Paolo is from Italy.

   _____

4. Anna is single.

   _____

5. The teachers are in the hall.

   _____

6. This country is very large.

   _____

7. Mr. Lee is from Korea.

   _____

C Write each sentence again. Use a contraction.

I am	→	I'm		I am not	→	I'm not
You are	→	You're		You are not	→	You aren't
We are	→	We're		We are not	→	We aren't
They are	→	They're		They are not	→	They aren't
He is	→	He's		He is not	→	He isn't
She is	→	She's		She is not	→	She isn't
It is	→	It's		It is not	→	It isn't

1. I am a student.   *I'm a student.*

2. You are from Spain.   _____

3. He is at work.   _____

4. She is twenty years old. _____

5. They are not married.   _____

6. We are students.   _____

7. It is in the classroom. _____

8. She is not in class today. _____

D Match each question with the correct answer.

__g__	**1.** Is your school small?	**a.** No, I'm not. I'm single.
_____	**2.** Are you a teacher?	**b.** Yes, we are.
_____	**3.** Is she from France?	**c.** Yes, it is. It's very large.
_____	**4.** Is this a large city?	**d.** No, he isn't. He's from Australia.
_____	**5.** Are you married?	**e.** No, I'm not. I'm at school.
_____	**6.** Are we hardworking students?	**f.** No, I'm not. I'm a student.
_____	**7.** Is your teacher from the US?	**g.** Yes, it is.
_____	**8.** Are you at work now?	**h.** Yes, she is.

E Write the questions that match each answer.

Are you married?	What's your address?
How old are you?	~~What's your name?~~
What country are you from?	What's your telephone number?

1. _What's your name?_ _____

My name is John Phillips.

2. _____

I live at 2375 Oak Hill Road.

3. _____

I'm from the United States.

4. _____

It's 555-6322.

5. _____

Yes, I am.

6. _____

I'm 33.

F Complete the questions and answers.

This is Pablo. He is from Mexico. He's 17 years old. Pablo is a student at Adams High School. He's at school now.

1. _____Is_____ Pablo from Mexico?   Yes, _____he_____ _____is_____.

2. _____ Pablo 19 years old?   No, _____ _____.

3. _____ he a student?   _____, _____ _____.

4. _____ _____ at home now?   _____, _____ _____.

G Complete the questions and answers.

This is Diego and his family. They are from Honduras. Diego is 40 years old. His wife, Ana, is 38 years old. They have two children. Junior is seven years old and Melissa is ten. Diego is at home now. The children are at school now.

1. _____Is_____ Diego married?   Yes, _____he_____ _____is_____.

2. _____ Diego and Ana from Mexico?   No, _____ _____.

3. _____ Ana 38 years old?   _____, _____ _____.

4. _____ Diego at work now?   _____, _____ _____.

5. _____ the children at school now?   _____, _____ _____.

H Write four additional questions and answers about the children.

This is Ava, and this is Adam. They are brother and sister. Adam is six and Ava is five. Adam is in first grade and Ava is in kindergarten. They are not at school. They are at home.

1. Are Adam and Ava brother and sister? _____   _____Yes, they are._____

2. _____   _____

3. _____   _____

4. _____   _____

5. _____   _____

LISTENING

I Listen to each person. Then, answer the questions. 🎧2

1. Who is from Uganda?   _____Eric_____
2. Who is from Peru?   _____Paula_____
3. Who is a teacher?   _____
4. Who goes to classes three nights a week?   _____
5. Who goes to a community college?   _____
6. Is Eric's school big?   _____
7. Is Eric's class big?   _____
8. Is Paula's school big?   _____

J Listen and circle each correct answer. 🎧3

1. **a.** My first name is Maria.   **b.** My last name is Jones.   **c.** My middle initial is R.
2. **a.** I'm from the US.   **b.** I'm from California.   **c.** I'm from San Francisco.
3. **a.** I'm a student.   **b.** No, I'm not.   **c.** No, I'm Italian.
4. **a.** I'm from Russia.   **b.** No, I'm Canadian.   **c.** I'm from Florida.
5. **a.** No, it's big.   **b.** Yes, I am.   **c.** No, I'm not.
6. **a.** It's 555-3973.   **b.** It's 1215 Park Street.   **c.** It's 05063.

K Listen and write the sentences. 🎧4

1. His name is Pablo. _____
2. _____
3. _____
4. _____
5. _____
6. _____
7. _____
8. _____

Jack Johnson

Jack Johnson is a musician, surfer, and environmentalist. He sings and plays the guitar. He uses music to teach people about saving the earth.

Jack's birthdate is May 18, 1975. He was born in Oahu, Hawaii. His father is a famous surfer. Jack learned how to surf when he was a child. He competed in surfing competitions as a teenager. He graduated from the University of California, Santa Barbara, in 1997. He married his college girlfriend, Kim. They have three children. Jack and Kim started a charity to help the arts and the environment in 2008. 🎧5

L Read each statement and circle *True* or *False*.

1.	Jack Johnson is a musician.	(True)	False
2.	He plays the violin.	True	False
3.	He uses music to teach people about the environment.	True	False
4.	His birthday is in May.	True	False
5.	He is from Los Angeles, California.	True	False
6.	He learned to surf as a teenager.	True	False
7.	His father is also a surfer.	True	False
8.	He and his wife started a charity.	True	False

A Label the numbered items in this classroom.

1. _____the floor_____   8. _____

2. _____   9. _____

3. _____   10. _____

4. _____   11. _____

5. _____   12. _____

6. _____   13. _____

7. _____   14. _____

B Look at the classroom on the previous page. Write the names of four more singular and plural items.

Singular	Plural
teacher	desks

C Complete these sentences about the classroom on the previous page.

There is a	There are
There isn't a	There aren't any

1. _____There are seven_____ students in this class.

2. _____ teacher in the front of the room.

3. _____ children in this class.

4. _____ women in this class.

5. _____ computers in this classroom.

6. _____ map on the wall.

7. _____ clock above the chalkboard.

8. _____ pencil sharpener in this room.

9. _____ bookcase in the room.

D Write five more sentences about the classroom on the previous page.

1. _____

2. _____

3. _____

4. _____

5. _____

E Plural nouns. Write the plural of each noun.

1. a city _____cities_____
2. a child _____
3. a clock _____
4. a pencil _____
5. a man _____
6. a school _____
7. an eraser _____

8. a class _____
9. a telephone _____
10. a library _____
11. a bus _____
12. a parking lot _____
13. a woman _____
14. an office _____

F Singular and plural nouns. Write *a* or *an* before each noun. If you do not need *a* or *an*, put an *X*.

1. _____an_____ office
2. _____X_____ students
3. _____a_____ dictionary
4. _____ bookstore
5. _____ English book
6. _____ restrooms
7. _____ classes
8. _____ class

9. _____ exam
10. _____ busy students
11. _____ empty classroom
12. _____ old desks
13. _____ computer center
14. _____ expensive book
15. _____ expensive books
16. _____ intelligent student

G Change each sentence from singular to plural. Use the number in parentheses.

1. There is a woman in the class. (six)

   There are six women in the class.

2. There is a computer in the computer lab. (twenty)

   _____

3. There is a dictionary in my backpack. (two)

   _____

4. There is an elevator in the building. (three)

   _____

5. There is a student in room 421. (fifteen)

   _____

H Answer the questions about this college campus. It is exam week and many students are studying in the library or taking exams.

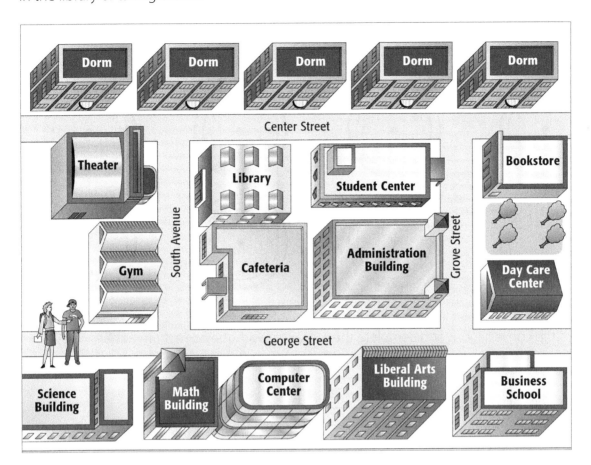

Yes, there is.	Yes, there are.
No, there isn't.	No, there aren't.

1. Is there a large library on campus? _____ *Yes, there is.* _____

2. Are there a lot of students in the library? _____

3. Are there many buildings on campus? _____

4. Is there a computer center on campus? _____

5. Is there a park next to the library? _____

6. Are there any students in the park? _____

7. Are there many students in the classrooms? _____

8. Are there five dorms on campus? _____

9. Is there a gym on campus? _____

10. Is there a student center next to the gym? _____

11. Are there many students outside today? _____

LISTENING

I Listen and draw the correct time on the clocks. 🎧6

a.

c.

e.

g.

b.

d.

f.

h.

J Listen to the conversations and complete the sentences with the correct time. 🎧7

1. Class begins at _____ *9:00* _____.

2. Class ends at _____.

3. The computer lab opens at _____.

4. Ms. Jackson is in her office from _____ to _____.

5. The bookstore is open from _____ to _____.

6. The library is open from _____ to _____.

K Listen. Then, answer the questions about this picture. 🎧8

Yes, there is.	Yes, there are.
No, there isn't.	No, there aren't.

1. _____ *No, there isn't.* _____

2. _____

3. _____

4. _____

5. _____

6. _____

7. _____

8. _____

9. _____

10. _____

L You will hear ten sentences about the items on this desk. Write the five sentences that are true.

🎧 9

1. _There is a dictionary on the desk._ _____

2. _____

3. _____

4. _____

5. _____

READING   Personal Narrative

My School

Anina: I go to an adult school in my city. In this school, we have three levels: beginning, intermediate, and advanced. Classes are on Monday and Wednesday night, from 7:00 to 9:00. The classes are free and our books are free. There are 40 students in my class.

Simon: I go to a private language school in my city. We can study in the morning, in the afternoon, or in the evening. I attend classes 15 hours a week. Classes are $100 a week. Our classes are very small, with five to ten students in a class.

Lili: I attend ESL classes at a community college in my city. In the intensive program, there are five levels. We have classes five days a week, four hours a day. There is also an ESL computer lab to use. In my class, there are 25 students. The tuition is $1,500 a semester. After I finish the top level, I can take regular college classes. 🎧 10

M Check (✓) the correct student or students for each sentence.

		Anina	**Simon**	**Lili**
1.	This student attends school 20 hours a week.	☐	☐	✓
2.	This student pays tuition.	☐	☐	☐
3.	This student attends school two days a week.	☐	☐	☐
4.	This student is in a big class.	☐	☐	☐
5.	This student is in a small class.	☐	☐	☐
6.	This student can use a computer lab.	☐	☐	☐

THE FAMILY

A Complete the sentences about the family. Use the words from the box.

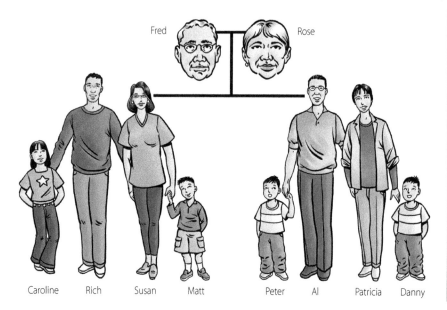

parents	grandparents
mother	grandmother
father	grandfather
wife	grandchildren
~~husband~~	granddaughter
children	grandson
daughter	aunt
son	uncle
sister	niece
brother	nephew
cousin	

Caroline   Rich   Susan   Matt   Peter   Al   Patricia   Danny

1. Fred is Rose's _____ husband _____.

2. Rose is Susan's _____.

3. Al is Susan's _____.

4. Caroline and Matt are Rich and Susan's _____.

5. Patricia is Al's _____.

6. Danny is Susan's _____.

7. Al is Caroline and Matt's _____.

8. Peter is Matt's _____.

9. Al and Patricia are Peter and Danny's _____.

10. Rose is Danny and Peter's _____.

11. Rose and Fred have four _____.

12. Rose and Fred are Caroline and Matt's _____.

B Read and answer the questions about the family on the previous page.

1. Who is Rich's son? _____ Matt _____

2. Who is Peter and Danny's grandfather? _____

3. Who is Rose's daughter? _____

4. Who is Danny and Peter's aunt? _____

5. Who is Caroline and Matt's uncle? _____

6. Who is Al's niece? _____

7. How many nephews does Susan have? _____

8. How many grandsons does Fred have? _____

9. How many cousins do Peter and Danny have? _____

10. How many daughters do Al and Patricia have? _____

11. Who is Rose's son-in-law? _____

12. Who is Rose's daughter-in-law? _____

C Answer the questions about your family.

1. How many brothers and sisters do you have? I have _____.

2. How many brothers do you have? _____.

3. How many sisters do you have? _____.

4. Are you married or single? I am _____.

5. What is your husband's / wife's name? My _____.

6. How many children do you have? _____.

7. How many sons do you have? _____.

8. How many daughters do you have? _____.

D Look at the picture on the previous page. Read the paragraph. Then, answer the question.

My father's name is Rich, and my mother's name is Susan. I have a brother. He's six years old. His name is Matt. I'm nine years old. My grandparents live next door. Their names are Grandpa Fred and Grandma Rose.

Who's talking? _____

E Complete the sentences using *she, her, he, his, they,* or *their.*

1. _____Her_____ name is Liliana. _____ is from Argentina. _____ works at a library. _____ lives with _____ family. _____ has two sons. _____ are 16 and 18 years old. _____ speak English very well.

2. _____ name is Vincent. _____ is from Oregon, and _____ is a college student. _____ is studying graphic design. _____ family is from Beijing, China.

3. _____ names are Jada, Erin, and Nicki. _____ are elementary school students. Jada and Erin are seven. _____ are in second grade. Nicki is eight. _____ is in third grade. _____ are sisters.

F Complete with *I, my, our, he,* or *we.*

This is _____my_____ best friend, Kabir. Kabir and _____ are college students. _____ study together. _____ class is in Room 412. _____ study English at a college in New York. _____ are from India. _____ am from Jaipur. _____ is from Delhi.

G Complete with the correct simple present form of the verb in parentheses and write the job.

1. Denise _____works_____ (work) as a _____teller_____ in a bank. She _____likes_____ (like) her job. She _____ (work) part time.

2. Marco _____ (work) as a _____ in a restaurant. He _____ (want) to work in a hotel.

3. Camila _____ (work) as a _____ in a high school. She _____ (like) her job. Her job _____ (be) part time. She _____ (want) to work full time.

4. Christine and Evan _____ (work) as _____ in a city hospital. They _____ (like) their jobs. They _____ (work) from 11:00 p.m. to 7:00 a.m., five days a week.

5. George _____ (work) as a _____ in a museum. He _____ (live) far from the museum, so he _____ (drive) to work. He _____ (walk) around the museum all day.

he she	drives
	likes
	lives
	walks
	wants
	works
they	drive
	like
	live
	walk
	want
	work

H Cross out the occupation in each group that does not belong.

1. teacher	~~artist~~	school bus driver	student
2. waitress	cook	teacher	waiter
3. lawyer	secretary	architect	bus driver
4. dentist	taxi driver	auto mechanic	bus driver
5. nurse	home health aide	cook	dentist
6. engineer	farmer	accountant	architect

LISTENING

I Listen and write the correct age below each family member. 🎧11

J Look at the picture in Exercise I. Listen to each description. Write the names of the family members. 🎧12

1. _____Masa_____

2. _____

3. _____

4. _____

5. _____

6. _____

K Listen and answer the questions about the picture. 🎧13

Joanne Gray: 29

1. _No, she isn't._
2. _____
3. _____
4. _____

L Listen and answer the questions about yourself. 🎧14

1. _____
2. _____
3. _____
4. _____

READING   Personal Story

Ana Velez

Ana Velez has a very large family. She has fifteen brothers and sisters! She has seven brothers and eight sisters. Ana is the oldest sister. She's 33 years old. Her oldest brother is 45, and her youngest sister is 20. There are two sets of twins—her brothers, Germán and José, and her sisters, Diana and Dina. Ana is married to Julio. Julio has a large family, too. He has six brothers, so Ana has six brothers-in-law! Ana is going to have her first child next month. She and Julio want a small family—a boy and a girl. 🎧15

M Circle *True* or *False*.

1.	Ana has a large family.	True	False
2.	Ana has eight brothers.	True	False
3.	Ana is the oldest. She's 45 years old.	True	False
4.	Germán and José are twins.	True	False
5.	Ana and Dina are twins.	True	False
6.	Ana's husband has a large family.	True	False
7.	Julio has a sister.	True	False
8.	Ana and Julio have two children.	True	False

A Look at the picture. Complete the sentences with the correct preposition. Some prepositions can be used more than once.

1. The sofa is _____in_____ the living room.

2. The end table is _____ the sofa.

3. The books are _____ the coffee table.

4. The picture is _____ the sofa.

5. The nightstand is _____ the dresser and the bed.

6. The table is _____ the kitchen.

7. The remote control is _____ the television.

8. The coffee table is _____ the sofa.

9. The bed is _____ the light.

10. The garbage can is _____ the sink.

| behind |
| between |
| in |
| in front of |
| next to |
| on |
| over |
| under |

B Answer these questions about the house on the previous page.

1. Where is the television?   It's on the small table.

2. Where is the lamp?

3. Where is the dresser?

4. Where is the toilet?

5. Where is the bathtub?

6. Where are the pillows?

7. Where is the toaster oven?

8. Where is the cat?

9. Where is the window in the living room?

10. Where are the shoes?

C Write ten questions and answers about this picture.

1. Where's the photo?   It's next to the lamp.

2.

3.

4.

5.

6.

7.

8.

9.

10.

D Complete the statements about the map. Use *can* and a verb from the box. Some verbs can be used more than once.

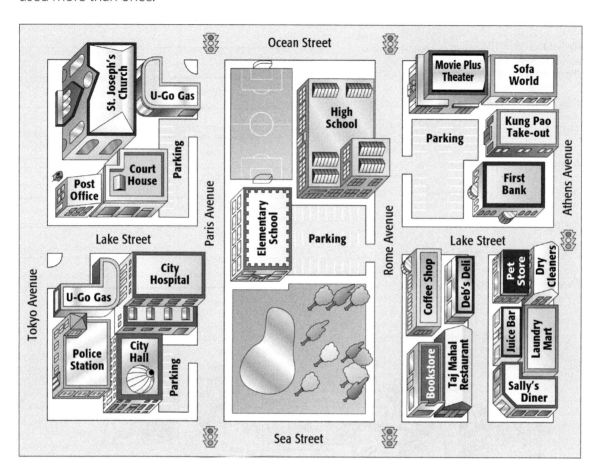

1. I _____can watch_____ a movie at the Movie Plus Theater.

2. I _____ my parking ticket at the police station.

3. We _____ gas at U-Go Gas.

4. You _____ a dictionary at the bookstore.

5. I _____ for English classes at the high school.

6. She _____ her clothes at Laundry Mart.

7. You _____ your car across from the high school.

8. I _____ in the park.

9. He _____ a sofa and armchair at Sofa World.

10. You _____ a letter at the post office.

buy

get

mail

park

pay

register

walk

wash

watch

E Complete the sentences about the map on the previous page with the correct prepositions. Some prepositions can be used more than once.

across from	in	on
behind	in front of	on the corner of
between	next to	

1. The high school is _____on_____ Rome Avenue.

2. The post office is _____ Tokyo Avenue and Lake Street.

3. Laundry Mart is _____ Sally's Diner and the dry cleaners.

4. Movie Plus Theater is _____ Ocean Street and Rome Avenue.

5. There is a parking lot _____ City Hall.

6. There is another parking lot _____ the high school.

7. There are many students _____ the high school.

8. The bookstore is _____ the Taj Mahal Restaurant.

9. The park is _____ the bookstore.

10. Deb's Deli is _____ the Taj Mahal Restaurant.

F Look at the map on the previous page and give the location of each building. Then, give the location of five more buildings on the map.

1. City Hospital is _on the corner of Lake Street and Paris Avenue._____

2. Kung Pao Take-out is _____

3. The dry cleaners is _____

4. St. Joseph's Church is _____

5. The Juice Bar is _____

6. _____

7. _____

8. _____

9. _____

10. _____

G Listen and write the questions about the kitchen. Then, answer each question. 🎧 16

1. <u>Where is the coffee maker?</u>   <u>It's on the counter.</u>

2. _____   _____

3. _____   _____

4. _____   _____

5. _____   _____

6. _____   _____

7. _____   _____

8. _____   _____

H Listen and write the name of each building. 🎧 17

~~barbershop~~	car wash	diner	jewelry store
bookstore	City Hall	hospital	library

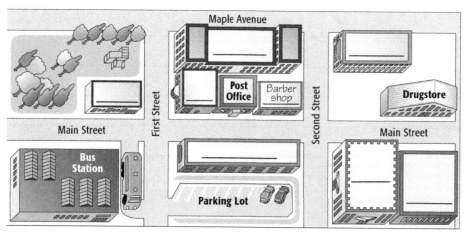

I Listen to the questions about an apartment for rent. Write the number of the question next to the correct answer. 🎧18

🏢 **For Rent**
• **One BR apt. in the city.**
• **Call or email for information.**

_____ No, no pets are allowed.

_____ Water and electric are included. You pay for heat.

___1___ It's on 14th Street.

_____ It's $1,100 a month.

_____ Yes, it's near the bus and the subway.

_____ No, there's no parking.

_____ It has one bedroom.

READING Descriptive Text

My Neighborhood

This is a photo of spices at a store in an Indian shopping area near my house. There are many Indian stores in my neighborhood. There are Indian grocery stores, bakeries, sari stores, and jewelry stores. There's also a hardware store. At the grocery stores, we can buy all of our favorite kinds of Indian pickles, such as mango pickles and Gujarati pickles. The fruits from India are similar to the fruits in this country, and those are at the grocery stores, too. In the sari stores, women can buy beautiful, long saris in many colors. Many Indian men and women like to wear jewelry, especially gold, so there are many jewelry stores. Saturday and Sunday are the busiest days on this street. Families from many towns come and shop in this area. Then, they enjoy a delicious lunch or dinner at one of the many Indian restaurants. 🎧19

J What can people do or buy in this shopping area?

1. People can _buy many different types of food._

2. People can _____

3. People can _____

4. People can _____

5. People can _____

UNIT 4 A TYPICAL DAY

A Complete each sentence with a verb or verbs from the box. Not all verbs will be used. Verbs may be used more than once.

drive	eat	exercise	~~get up~~	read	relax	take	walk	watch	work
drives	eats	exercises	gets up	reads	relaxes	takes	walks	watches	works

1. Susan and Peter
_____*get* up_____
at 6:00.

2. Every morning, Susan
_____ and
Peter _____ a
shower.

3. At 7:30, Susan and Peter
_____
breakfast.

4. Susan _____
to work, but Peter
_____
to work.

5. Susan _____
in an office as a secretary.
Peter _____
for a construction company.

6. At 6:00, Susan and
Peter _____
dinner.

7. At 7:00, they _____
classes at a community college.

8. After school, they _____
at home. Susan _____ and
Peter _____ TV.

B Read each sentence. Circle the correct verb.

1. Susan **get up / gets up** at 6:00.

2. Peter **use / uses** the bathroom first.

3. He **take / takes** a shower and **get / gets** dressed for work.

4. Susan and Peter always **eat / eats** breakfast together.

5. They **like / likes** to talk about their plans for the day.

6. Susan **work / works** fifteen minutes from their home.

7. She **take / takes** her lunch to work.

8. Peter **like / likes** to eat lunch at a restaurant with coworkers.

9. On rainy days, Peter **pick / picks** Susan up after work, and they **ride / rides** home together.

C Look at Hugo's schedule. Complete each sentence about Hugo with the affirmative or the negative form of the verb in parentheses. Then, complete the sentences about yourself.

1. Hugo _____ *doesn't work* _____ (work) on Thursdays.

2. Hugo _____ (go) to the gym once a week.

3. He _____ (take) a class every night.

4. He _____ (eat) at home on Fridays.

5. He _____ (study) on Thursday nights.

6. Hugo _____ (go) dancing with his wife every night.

7. I _____ (work) on Thursday nights.

8. I _____ (go) to the gym once a week.

9. I _____ (take) classes five nights a week.

D Read each statement. Rewrite each sentence using a negative form. Then, write a true statement about yourself.

1. I get up at 4:00 a.m.

I don't get up at 4:00 a.m.

I get up at 7:00 a.m.

2. My English class begins at 2:00 p.m.

_____

_____

3. I study English six days a week.

_____

_____

4. My classmates and I do our homework together.

_We_ _____

_____

5. I always eat lunch at 11:00 a.m.

_____

_____

6. My family and I go on three trips a year.

_____

_____

7. Our teacher gives tests twice a week.

_____

_____

8. This school has classes on Sundays.

_____

_____

E Put the words in the correct order.

Adverbs of Frequency	
100%	always
80–90%	usually
60–70%	often
50%	sometimes
0%	never

1. at / usually / I / get up / 7:00 a.m.

   <u>I usually *get up at 7:00 a.m.*</u>

2. never / on time / She / for class / is

   _____

3. speak / students / always / English / in class / The

   _____

4. videos / watch / sometimes / in class / We

   _____

5. do / class / We / our homework / usually / before

   _____

6. a week / go / to the computer lab / once / The students

   _____

F Read and answer the questions using expressions from the box.

every day
every morning
every night
every summer
every year
never
once a month
once a week
three times a week
twice a week

1. How often do you go to the movies?

   _____

2. How often do you eat out?

   _____

3. How often do you go to the park?

   _____

4. How often do you drive to school?

   _____

5. How often does your class have tests?

   _____

6. How often does your teacher give homework?

   _____

7. How often does your English class meet?

   _____

G Final *s*. Listen and write the words in the correct column. 🎧20

/s/	/z/	/əz/
visits	buys	exercises

H Listen to Vicky's weekday schedule. Complete her schedule with the correct times and verbs. 🎧21

Time	Activity
In the daytime	
_____ 6:00 _____	— gets up
_____–_____	— runs
_____–_____	— takes a shower; gets dressed
_____	— eats breakfast
_____	— goes to work
_____–_____	— works
_____–_____	— eats lunch
_____	— gets home and checks her email
In the evening	

She likes to _____ TV, _____, or _____ time with friends.

_____–_____	— goes to yoga class _____ times a week
_____	— watches the news
_____	— goes to bed

I Listen and answer the questions about Vicky's schedule. 🎧22

1. <u>She gets up at 6:00.</u>

2. _____

3. _____

4. _____

5. _____

6. _____

READING   A Schedule

A Typical Day

Maya is a new doctor at a city hospital. She is married. She and her husband, Jake, have a five-year-old daughter named Judi. Maya works six days a week, Monday to Saturday. Sometimes she works on Sunday, too.

On a typical day, Maya gets up at 5:30 a.m., takes a shower, and gets dressed for work. She wakes Judi up and helps her get dressed. When her husband comes back from running, Maya goes to work. She buys coffee and a yogurt on the way to work. She starts work at 7:00 a.m. Maya works in the emergency room. She eats lunch at the diner across the street if she has free time.

Maya is very tired at the end of the day. Sometimes, she finishes at 6:00 p.m. and has dinner with her family. But, many days the head doctor says, "Maya, we need you to work late." She works late three or more times a week. When she gets home, everyone is already in bed. 🎧23

J Read each sentence. Correct the incorrect information about the story.

1. Maya works from ~~Tuesday~~ to Saturday.   <u> Monday </u>

2. Maya gets up at 7:30 a.m.   _____

3. Maya buys a green tea and a yogurt for breakfast.   _____

4. She works in the intensive care unit.   _____

5. She has dinner with her family every day.   _____

6. Maya never works late.   _____

UNIT 5 AIRPORT JOBS

A Answer the *Who* questions about airport jobs. Use the words from the box.

| aircraft mechanic |
| baggage handler |
| cabin cleaner |
| flight attendant |
| food prep worker |
| parking lot attendant |
| passenger service worker |
| pilot |
| ~~reservation agent~~ |
| security screener |

1. Who sells tickets? _A reservation agent does._
2. Who flies the plane? _____
3. Who repairs engines? _____
4. Who puts luggage on the plane? _____
5. Who prepares meals? _____
6. Who serves meals on the plane? _____
7. Who screens passengers? _____
8. Who collects parking fees? _____
9. Who drives people in the airport? _____
10. Who cleans the plane? _____

B Answer the questions.

| Yes, he does. | Yes, she does. | Yes, I do. |
| No, he doesn't. | No, she doesn't. | No, I don't. |

Jacob

Olga

1. Does Jacob wear a uniform? _Yes, he does._
2. Does he have a stressful job? _____
3. Do you have a stressful job? _____
4. Does Jacob have a high-paying job? _____
5. Does he stand all day? _____
6. Does Olga work outside? _____
7. Do you work outside? _____
8. Does Olga have an interesting job? _____
9. Does she serve meals? _____
10. Does she use a computer? _____

C Answer the questions about work benefits.

	Medical	**Dental**	**Prescription**	**Sick Days**	**Vacation**	**Retirement**
Sam	✓	✓	✓	10	3 weeks	
Marta	✓			7	2 weeks	
Ela	✓	✓		5	1 week	✓
Boris				3	1 week	

1. Does Sam have medical benefits? _____ *Yes, he does.* _____

2. Does Boris have a retirement plan? _____

3. Do all the workers have medical benefits? _____

4. Do you have medical benefits? _____

5. Do Sam and Ela have dental plans? _____

6. Does Sam have a prescription plan? _____

7. Do you have a prescription plan? _____

8. Does Marta have seven sick days? _____

9. Do you have sick days? _____

10. Does Sam have three weeks' vacation? _____

11. Do you have three weeks' vacation? _____

12. Do you have a retirement plan? _____

D Ask Luis about his job as a cook. Write the question for each answer.

Luis

1. _____ *Do you work full time?* _____ Yes, I work full time.

2. _____ Yes, I wear a uniform.

3. _____ Yes, I get medical benefits.

4. _____ No, I don't have a dental plan.

5. _____ No, I don't have a retirement plan.

6. _____ Yes, I like my job.

7. _____ Yes, I stand all evening.

E Match the questions and answers about Sonia's job as a food prep worker.

___f___ **1.** What do you do?

_____ **2.** Where do you work?

_____ **3.** What days do you work?

_____ **4.** What hours do you work?

_____ **5.** Do you work on Wednesdays?

_____ **6.** Do you wear a uniform?

_____ **7.** Is your boss helpful?

_____ **8.** What language do you speak at work?

_____ **9.** What company do you work for?

_____ **10.** Is the pay good?

a. I work from 6:00 a.m. to 2:00 p.m.

b. Everyone speaks Spanish.

c. No, the pay is low.

d. Yes, my boss is very nice.

e. I work at the Miami Airport.

f. I'm a food prep worker.

g. I work for Green Foods.

h. No, I don't.

i. I work from Thursday to Tuesday.

j. No, I don't wear a uniform.

F Read about David's job. Then, write the question for each answer.

David

My name is David and I'm a security screener at the Denver Airport. I screen passengers when they enter the boarding area. I also screen their luggage. I wear a blue uniform. I work the evening shift from 3:00 p.m. to 11:00 p.m. I usually work from Tuesday to Saturday. I sometimes work overtime. I have medical benefits and three sick days. I also have two weeks' vacation.

1. _____What do you do?_____ I'm a security screener.

2. _____ I work at the Denver Airport.

3. _____ I work from Tuesday to Saturday.

4. _____ I work from 3:00 p.m. to 11:00 p.m.

5. _____ I speak English.

6. _____ Yes, I wear a uniform.

7. _____ The pay is OK.

8. _____ Yes, I get medical benefits.

9. _____ Yes, I sometimes work overtime.

10. _____ Yes, I like my job.

G Write the questions from the box next to the correct answer.

Anna

> Does she like her job?
>
> Does she wear a uniform?
>
> Does she work part time?
>
> What are her hours?
>
> ~~What does Anna do?~~
>
> What language does she speak?
>
> Where does she work?

1. _____What does Anna do?_____   She's a parking lot attendant.

2. _____   She works at the Seattle Airport.

3. _____   No, she works full time.

4. _____   She works from 12:00 p.m. to 8:00 p.m.

5. _____   Yes, she wears a uniform.

6. _____   She speaks English.

7. _____   Yes, she does.

H Write seven questions and answers about Len's job.

Len

Len is a reservation agent for Western Airlines. He works at the Tulsa Airport. He works at the ticket counter and helps passengers. He checks their tickets and takes their baggage. He also sells tickets to passengers. Len works from Tuesday to Saturday and has Sunday and Monday off. He works from 6:00 a.m. to 2:00 p.m. He's always busy and there is always a long line of passengers at the ticket counter. Len makes a good salary and has medical benefits. He also gets free tickets if there are empty seats on a flight. Len likes his job a lot.

1. _____What does Len do?_____   _____He's a reservation agent._____

2. _____   _____

3. _____   _____

4. _____   _____

5. _____   _____

6. _____   _____

7. _____   _____

8. _____   _____

LISTENING

I Listen and complete the information about each job. 🎧 24

Beata

Job: _____ *baggage handler* _____

Airport: _____

Days: _____

Hours: _____

Salary: _____

Medical benefits: Yes   No

Dental plan: Yes   No

Sick days: _____ days

Vacation: _____ days

Ivan

Job: _____

Airport: _____

Days: _____

Hours: _____

Salary: _____

Medical benefits: Yes   No

Dental plan: Yes   No

Sick days: _____ days

Vacation: _____ days

J Listen to the questions about Beata's and Ivan's jobs. Circle the correct answer. 🎧 25

1. **a.** She's a baggage handler.   **b.** She works from 6:00 a.m. to 2:00 p.m.

2. **a.** Orlando.   **b.** Yes, she works at the airport.

3. **a.** From 6:00 a.m. to 2:00 p.m.   **b.** From Tuesday to Saturday.

4. **a.** Eight hours a day.   **b.** $12.00 an hour.

5. **a.** Yes, she does.   **b.** No, she doesn't.

6. **a.** She has four.   **b.** She has five.

7. **a.** He's an electric-cart driver.   **b.** He works at the Las Vegas Airport.

8. **a.** Yes, he does.   **b.** No, he doesn't.

9. **a.** Friday and Saturday.   **b.** Sunday to Thursday.

10. **a.** $8.00 an hour.   **b.** $15.00 an hour.

11. **a.** No, he doesn't.   **b.** Yes, he does.

12. **a.** He has six.   **b.** He has ten.

K You are applying for a job as a reservation agent. Listen and write the interview questions you hear. Then, answer the questions. 🎧26

1. _Are you working now_____? _____.

2. _____? _____.

3. _____? _____.

4. _____?

   _____.

5. _____?

   _____.

6. _____? _____.

7. _____? _____.

READING   Online Job Postings

CUSTODIAN—Full time in East River Schools. Should have experience with light electric and plumbing repair. Evening hours: 2 p.m. to 10 p.m. Medical benefits and two weeks' vacation. Email your resume and cover letter to careers@east*river.edu.	**SECURITY SCREENER**—Southside Airport. Full time. Must be available Sat. & Sun. Will train. Good benefits package including medical benefits. Bilingual a plus. Email your application to jobs@south*side.com or apply in person. Personnel Dept. Southside Airport.	**EXECUTIVE ASSISTANT**—Busy accounting office. Monday to Friday, 8:00 a.m. to 1:00 p.m. Answer phone, take messages, and schedule appointments. Computer skills and word processing required. Send your application to hr@angelo*accounting.com.
1.	**2.**	**3.** 🎧27

L Read the statements. Complete the chart about the three online job postings.

	Job 1	Job 2	Job 3
This job is full time.	✓	✓	
You need experience for this job.			
You have to work on weekends.			
You need to speak English well.			
You need computer skills for this job.			
This job offers medical benefits.			
You can apply in person for this job.			

A Complete the sentences with the present continuous form of each verb.

cut	go	install	look at	pack	wash
drive	greet	load	open	~~paint~~	wear

1. Their daughter _____is painting_____ her bedroom light yellow.

2. The landscapers _____ the grass.

3. Our electrician _____ two new lights.

4. The housekeepers _____ the windows.

5. The custodian _____ a brown uniform.

6. Martin and Dave _____ forklifts.

7. It's 8:30 a.m. Jean and Mario _____ their coworkers.

8. Violet _____ her new schedule.

9. Luisa and her coworkers _____ boxes and putting the new equipment on the table.

10. Jimmy _____ to the break room. He has a fifteen-minute break.

11. The workers in the warehouse _____ TVs into boxes.

12. David and three other coworkers _____ the boxes onto the delivery trucks.

B Look at the pictures. Circle the correct answers.

1. Marie **is carrying** / **is not carrying** a cup of coffee.

2. She **is taking** / **is not taking** the bus to work.

3. She **is driving** / **is not driving** to work.

4. She **is wearing** / **is not wearing** a uniform.

5. The workers **are taking / are not taking** a break.

6. They **are packing / are not packing** boxes.

7. They **are wearing / are not wearing** uniforms.

8. They **are using / are not using** machines.

C Look at the pictures and answer the questions.

1. What is she doing?

   She is talking to her coworkers.

2. What is she wearing?

   _____

3. What are they doing?

   _____

4. What are they doing?

   _____

5. What is he doing?

   _____

6. What is she reading?

   _____

D Complete the sentences about the picture and about yourself using the verbs in parentheses. Some sentences are negative.

1. The man _____is working_____ (work) outside.

2. He _____ (use) a mower.

3. He _____ (wear) earphones.

4. He _____ (wear) a hat.

5. I _____ (wear) a uniform.

6. I _____ (work) now.

7. I _____ (study) English.

8. I _____ (write) in my workbook.

9. I _____ (talk) to a classmate.

10. I _____ (listen) to music.

E Match the occupation with the equipment or job responsibilities.

___e___ 1. A construction worker | **a.** connects TVs to cable systems.

_____ 2. A packer | **b.** cleans floors and washes windows.

_____ 3. A custodian | **c.** paints rooms and buildings.

_____ 4. A cook | **d.** fixes lights and electrical problems.

_____ 5. A landscaper | **e.** builds houses.

_____ 6. A painter | **f.** prepares food.

_____ 7. An electrician | **g.** packs items into boxes.

_____ 8. A cable installer | **h.** cuts grass and plants flowers.

F Write a story about the people in the picture. What are their occupations? What are they wearing? What are they doing at the house?

build
deck
deliver
fix
garage
install
mow
paint
plant
repair
roof
tree

_____

_____

_____

_____

_____

_____

_____

_____

_____

_____

_____

LISTENING

G Listen and label the workers at Best TV. 🎧 **28**

Anna
Gene
Gloria
Hector
Joseph
Louise
Marie
Mei-Lin
Paul
Victor
Vladimir

H Listen and circle each correct answer. 🎧 **29**

1.	**a.** Victor is.	**b.** Louise is.	**c.** Marie is.
2.	**a.** Mei-Lin is.	**b.** Paul is.	**c.** Anna is.
3.	**a.** Marie is.	**b.** Gene is.	**c.** Both a and b
4.	**a.** Paul is.	**b.** Hector is.	**c.** Vladimir is.
5.	**a.** Gloria is.	**b.** Joseph is.	**c.** Vladimir is.
6.	**a.** Hector is.	**b.** Marie is.	**c.** Anna and Mei-Lin are.
7.	**a.** Hector is.	**b.** The manager is.	**c.** Joseph is.

I Listen and write the answers to the questions. 🎧 **30**

1. _She's drinking a cup of tea._

2. _____

3. _____

4. _____

5. _____

6. _____

Conversation 1				Conversation 2		
1. Gloria is filling out an application.	Yes	(No)		**1.** Victor is taking a break.	Yes	No
2. Joseph is looking for a new job.	Yes	No		**2.** Victor's boss is angry.	Yes	No
3. He wants to be a manager.	Yes	No		**3.** The company is quiet.	Yes	No

READING   An Article About Future Plans

Career Opportunities

Angela is working hard today. [1]She works at a large toy company, and it's very busy in the warehouse. Angela is a packer. She packs toys into large boxes. Angela's job is not difficult, but she must work quickly. It's summer, and this is a busy time of the year at the warehouse. All the new toys must be ready for fall and the winter holiday shopping season.

Angela likes her work schedule. She works from Monday to Friday, from 8:30 to 4:30. It's busy now, so she is working more hours. She works late, until 7:30, two nights a week, and works from 8:30 to 12:00 on Saturday morning. The company pays overtime when she works late or on Saturdays.

Right now, Angela is on her lunch break, and she is filling out an application on her laptop. She is typing her name, address, telephone number, and work experience. She is also typing the name of her high school and college. Angela is a part-time student at the local college. She is studying business management. This is her last semester in college, and there are many good opportunities in other areas of the toy company for employees with college experience. She wants to enter a training program for future store managers. The next training program begins in the fall. It takes two years to complete the program. This year's trainees are working in a store and studying store management in company classes. Maybe in the fall, Angela will be a trainee, too. 🎧32

K Find the answers in the reading. Underline and number each answer.

1. Where does Angela work?	**7.** What is Angela typing?
2. What is her job?	**8.** What is she studying?
3. What does she do at work?	**9.** Why does she want to work at the toy company?
4. Why is the company busy?	**10.** When is the next training program?
5. What days does Angela work?	**11.** How many years is the program?
6. What hours does she work?	**12.** What are the trainees doing this year?

A Answer the questions about the three friends and about yourself.

| Yes, she is. | Yes, they are. | Yes, I am. |
| No, she isn't. | No, they aren't. | No, I'm not. |

1. Are Mary, Vera, and Patricia eating out? _____ *Yes, they are.* _____

2. Are they talking? _____

3. Is Mary eating eggs? _____

4. Is Mary drinking a cup of coffee? _____

5. Are all the women drinking tea? _____

6. Is Patricia drinking coffee? _____

7. Is Patricia working at this restaurant? _____

8. Is Vera drinking a glass of juice? _____

9. Is Vera eating two donuts? _____

10. Is Vera eating eggs? _____

11. Are you eating now? _____

12. Are you drinking a cup of coffee now? _____

B Crystal is a delivery truck driver. She and her coworker, Ronaldo, are ordering lunch at a drive-through window. Put the words of the questions in the correct order. Then, answer the questions.

1. driving / Crystal / a / Is / car / ?

   Is Crystal driving a car?   No, she isn't.

2. Crystal / their / lunch break / taking / Are / Ronaldo / and / ?

   _____   _____

3. a / sandwich / Crystal / ordering / chicken / Is / ?

   _____   _____

4. Ronaldo / wearing / uniforms / Are / their / Crystal / and / ?

   _____   _____

5. waiting / in / they / Are / long / a / line / ?

   _____   _____

6. cashier / talking / Crystal / to / the / Is / ?

   _____   _____

7. handing / Crystal / the / cashier / Is / twenty dollars / ?

   _____   _____

8. delivering / Are / a package / to / restaurant / they / this / ?

   _____   _____

C Write the correct question next to each picture. Then, write an answer.

> What are they eating?
>
> What are they looking at?
>
> What is Alex doing?
>
> What is Alex ordering to drink?
>
> What is Luz ordering?
>
> ~~Where are Luz and Alex sitting?~~

1. Where are Luz and Alex sitting?

They are sitting in a restaurant.

2. _____

_____

3. _____

_____

4. _____

_____

5. _____

_____

6. _____

_____

D Answer these *Who* questions about Coffee to Go.

1. Who is paying for an order? _____ Mr. Lopez is. _____

2. Who is wearing a uniform? _____

3. Who is talking to Vince? _____

4. Who is wearing a baseball cap? _____

5. Who is standing in front of Pamela? _____

6. Who is wearing glasses? _____

E Look at the picture in Exercise D. Write the question for each answer.

1. *How much is Mr. Lopez's order?* _____ His order is $3.00.

2. _____ He's pouring a cup of coffee.

3. _____ Yes, she is.

4. _____ They are wearing uniforms.

5. _____ Pamela is.

6. _____ Four customers.

7. _____ Behind the counter.

F Rewrite each sentence with *'d like*.

1. **I want** a salad. *I'd like a salad.* _____

2. **She wants** chicken nuggets. _____

3. **He wants** a medium coffee. _____

4. **We want** a medium cheese pizza. _____

5. **They want** two hot dogs. _____

G Listen and complete the prices on the menu. 🎧33

Lunch Menu

Sandwiches

Tuna salad sandwich	$ 7.99
Chicken salad sandwich	$
Roast beef sandwich	$
Turkey sandwich	$
Hamburger & french fries	$
Cheeseburger & french fries	$
Grilled cheese sandwich	$

Salads

Chef's salad	$
Small salad	$

Soups

Vegetable soup	$
Soup of the day	$

Beverages

Coffee, tea	$
Iced tea	$
Soda	$

Desserts

Ice cream	$
Cake	$

H Listen to these conversations between a waitress and four different customers. Write the number of the order under each picture. 🎧34

_____   _____   _____   _____

I Use the menu in Exercise G. How much is the bill for each order in Exercise H?

Order 1: _____   Order 3: _____

Order 2: _____   Order 4: _____

J Listen to these questions you hear at restaurants. Circle the correct answers. 🎧35

1. **a.** Yes, please.   **b.** Thank you.   **c.** Good morning.

2. **a.** Thank you.   **b.** A hamburger.   **c.** A small soda.

3. **a.** Large, please.   **b.** Nothing.   **c.** A cola.

4. **a.** To go.   **b.** A small order of fries.   **c.** Small.

5. **a.** That's all.   **b.** For here.   **c.** How much is that?

6. **a.** Large.   **b.** No sugar.   **c.** Regular.

7. **a.** Two sugars.   **b.** Small.   **c.** Nothing else.

8. **a.** Large, please.   **b.** Three donuts.   **c.** Two packets.

9. **a.** One.   **b.** A chocolate donut.   **c.** To go.

10. **a.** Small.   **b.** Veggie.   **c.** Two.

READING   Informational Text

Portions

In the United States, many people are **unhealthy**. Some experts say restaurant **portions** in the US are too big, and that there's too much fat and salt in the food. Many restaurants are now offering other **options**, or choices, for their customers.

It is easy to eat too much at a restaurant. You can order just one hamburger, but most food is ordered as a "meal." One kind of meal is a hamburger, french fries, and a soda. At many fast-food restaurants, you can get larger portions for only a dollar more. You'll receive an extra large order of fries and an extra large soda. That means the meal **contains** more calories, more fat, and more sugar.

Today, most restaurants **offer** healthy choices. They offer salads with low-calorie dressings, non-fat or **reduced**-fat milk, water, and chicken that is grilled instead of fried. So now customers have healthy options. 🎧36

K Match each word from the reading with its meaning.

___d___ **1.** unhealthy   **a.** meal size

_____ **2.** portions   **b.** choices

_____ **3.** options   **c.** has

_____ **4.** contains   **d.** not in good health

_____ **5.** offer   **e.** less

_____ **6.** reduced   **f.** sell

GOOD WEEKEND / BAD WEEKEND

A Where was each person last Saturday? Answer the questions.

1. Where was Gina?

She was at the gym.

2. Where were Tony and Evan?

_____

3. Where were Susan and her sisters?

_____

4. Where was George?

_____

5. Where was Kevin?

_____

6. Where was Sandra?

_____

7. Where was Peter?

_____

8. Where were Cindy and Charles?

_____

B Change the sentences from the present to the past.

1. She is late for class.   _She was late for class._

2. He is at the store.   _____

3. They are at the library.   _____

4. I am home.   _____

5. You are busy.   _____

6. The children are noisy.   _____

7. The price is high.   _____

8. The weather is cloudy.   _____

9. We are on vacation.   _____

10. I am tired.   _____

C Complete the sentences with *was* or *were* and the correct preposition of time.

in	on	at	from...to...
year: in 2018 month: in June season: in the summer in the morning in the afternoon in the evening	day: on Monday date: on June 4 on the weekend	time: at 4:00 at noon at midnight at night	from Monday to Friday from 1:00 to 3:00

1. The party was at ____was____ ____at____ 8:00.

2. The boys _____ at the movies _____ the evening.

3. The meeting _____ _____ Monday _____ 2:00.

4. We _____ in Detroit _____ April.

5. The boss _____ out of the office _____ Monday _____ Wednesday.

6. I _____ in New Mexico _____ the winter.

7. We _____ at church _____ 9:00 _____ the morning.

8. I _____ in my native country _____ August.

9. She _____ born _____ October 27, 1995.

10. The students _____ in the library _____ 3:00 _____ 6:00.

D Complete the questions and answers about a bad flight.

delayed = late

1. _____Was_____ the flight on time?

   No, ____it wasn't____. ____It was delayed____.

2. _____ the plane empty?

   No, _____. It _____ crowded.

3. _____ the seats comfortable?

   No, _____. They _____.

4. _____ the food good?

   No, _____. It _____.

5. _____ the weather good?

   No, _____. It _____.

6. _____ the bathrooms clean?

   No, _____. They _____.

E Put the words in the conversation in the correct order.

1. vacation / your / was / How / ?

How was your vacation?

2. wonderful / was / It

_____

3. you / Where / were / ?

_____

4. beach / at / the / were / We

_____

5. were / How long / there / you / ?

_____

6. there / for / were / a month / We

_____

7. the / How / weather / was / ?

_____

8. sunny / was / and / It / hot

_____

F Complete the questions.

Larry: _____ _Where were you_ _____ last night?

Jack: We were at a basketball game.

Larry: Where _____?

Jack: It was at King Arena.

Larry: How _____?

Jack: The game was great!

Larry: Where _____?

Jack: Our seats were in the tenth row.

Larry: How much _____?

Jack: The tickets were $20 each.

G Listen to each statement about school. (Circle) *present* or *past*. 🎧37

1.	(present)	past	**7.**	present	past
2.	present	past	**8.**	present	past
3.	present	past	**9.**	present	past
4.	present	past	**10.**	present	past
5.	present	past	**11.**	present	past
6.	present	past	**12.**	present	past

H Listen and write the question for each answer. 🎧38

1. _Where was Jack?_____

He was at the dentist's.

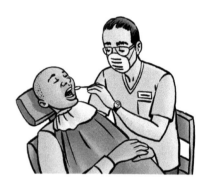

2. _____

He was there because he had a toothache.

3. _____

It was $150.

4. _____

No, she was home.

5. _____

She had the flu.

6. _____

She was in bed all week.

7. _____

She was in Hawaii.

8. _____

She was there for two weeks.

9. _____

It was sunny and hot.

I Listen and complete the questions with *is*, *are*, *was*, or *were*. Then, answer the questions. 🎧39

1. _____Are_____ you a student?   _____Yes, I am._____

2. _____ you a student last year? _____

3. _____ you in class now? _____

4. _____ you at home? _____

5. _____ you at school last night? _____

6. _____ your teacher absent yesterday? _____

7. _____ you a good student? _____

8. _____ the last test difficult? _____

9. _____ the homework difficult? _____

10. _____ this your first English class? _____

READING   Receipts

J Luis and Carmen enjoyed a short weekend vacation. Look at the receipts and complete the information. Use your imagination.

Ocean View Motel

Date: August 17

Arrive	:	August 15
Depart	:	August 17
Double Room	:	$112.00
Double Room	:	$112.00
Sales Tax	:	$ 13.44
City Tax	:	$ 20.16
Total	:	$257.60

The Mayfair

Date: August 16

Appetizers	:	$11.00
Dinners	:	$42.00
Drinks	:	$12.00
Dessert	:	$10.00
Tax	:	$ 4.50
Total	:	$79.50
Tip	:	$15.00

The Fish House

Date: August 15

2 House Salads	:	$10.00
2 Shrimp Dinners	:	$38.00
Drinks	:	$10.00
Tax	:	$ 3.48
Total	:	$61.48
Tip	:	$ 8.00

1. Luis and Carmen were at the _____beach_____ last weekend.

2. They liked their room at the Ocean View Motel because it was _____ and _____.

3. They were at the motel for _____ nights.

4. Their room was _____ a night.

5. The city tax for their room was _____.

6. The meal at _____ was more expensive.

7. Their shrimp dinner at _____ was delicious.

8. The service was excellent at the _____, but the food at the _____ was better.

A What did these people do last weekend? Use the simple past form the word box.

clean	listen	~~talk~~	wash
cook	study	walk	watch

1. ___She talked to her friend.___

5. _____

2. _____

6. _____

3. _____

7. _____

4. _____

8. _____

B What did these people do last weekend? Write the simple past form of the irregular verbs in the box. Then, use an irregular verb to describe each picture.

go	_____went_____	sleep	_____
read	_____	drink	_____
drive	_____	make	_____
do	_____	eat	_____

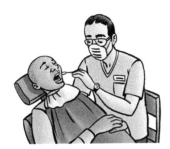

1. _____He went to the dentist._____

5. _____

2. _____

6. _____

3. _____

7. _____

4. _____

8. _____

C Complete the story. Write each verb in the simple past form.

My little sister is ten years old. Yesterday _____ was _____ (be) her birthday. In the morning, I _____ (go) to the mall and _____ (buy) her a light blue sweater and a pair of jeans. In the afternoon, my mom _____ (cook) her favorite dinner and I _____ (make) a chocolate birthday cake. At 6:00, her three best friends _____ (arrive). We all _____ (enjoy) a great dinner. Then, we _____ (bring) in the cake and we _____ (sing) "Happy Birthday." She _____ (love) all her presents.

After dinner, I _____ (take) the girls to see a new movie at the local theater. Then, the girls _____ (have) a sleepover. They _____ (stay) up until 2:00 in the morning! My sister _____ (have) a great birthday.

D Answer each question. Use the simple past.

1. What did you eat for lunch?   I _____ ate _____ a sandwich.

2. How did you feel?   I _____ tired.

3. When did you lose your wallet?   I _____ it yesterday.

4. What book did you read?   I _____ *Jane Eyre.*

5. What did you give your mother?   I _____ her some flowers.

6. What did she make for dinner?   She _____ lasagna.

7. Where did you meet your wife?   I _____ her at a party.

8. What did you think about the movie?   I _____ it was boring.

9. When did they get married?   They _____ married in 2004.

10. When did he come to the US?   He _____ in 2010.

11. What did she say?   She _____ ,"I'm sorry."

12. When did you take the test?   I _____ it yesterday.

13. Did you know all the answers?   Yes. I _____ all the answers.

14. How did you hear the news?   I _____ it online.

15. When did they leave?   They _____ at 11:00.

E Match each problem to the correct reason.

_____c_____ **1.** He didn't wash the dishes

_____ **2.** He couldn't return his sweater

_____ **3.** He had to pay a late fee

_____ **4.** He missed the bus

_____ **5.** He was tired all day

_____ **6.** Someone stole his car

_____ **7.** He didn't do his homework

_____ **8.** He's very hungry

a. because he didn't pay his bill on time.

b. because he didn't get enough sleep.

c. because he didn't have any soap.

d. because he didn't eat lunch.

e. because he didn't keep the receipt.

f. because he didn't have his book.

g. because he didn't get up on time.

h. because he didn't lock it.

Now, complete these sentences. Use didn't in your answer.

9. He failed the test because _____.

10. The police officer gave him a ticket because _____.

11. The boss fired him because _____.

F Everyone in this family was busy on Saturday morning. Write a story about this picture using the simple past.

_____

_____

_____

_____

_____

G Listen to the questions. Complete the sentences with simple past verbs. 🎧 40

1. I _____ saw _____ it last night.

2. I _____ a watch.

3. He _____ to the park.

4. They _____ at 2:00.

5. He _____ his books.

6. She _____ to Texas.

7. I _____ $100.

8. He _____ a cup of coffee.

9. I _____ at the library.

10. They _____ to the city.

11. I _____ a sweater.

12. He _____ his arm.

13. It _____ at 10:00.

14. I _____ it yesterday.

15. I _____ seven hours.

16. I _____ $50.

H Listen and write each sentence next to the pictures. 🎧 41

1. Yesterday, there was a big shoe sale. _____

2. _____

3. _____

4. _____

5. _____

6. _____

7. _____

8. _____

9. _____

10. _____

11. _____

12. _____

I Where did the person go last weekend? Listen to each question and write the place. 🎧42

1. _____post office_____
2. _____
3. _____
4. _____
5. _____

6. _____
7. _____
8. _____
9. _____
10. _____

READING   Short Story

Where's my car?

Last weekend, my wife and I went to our first major league baseball game at a large stadium in the city. One of my friends gave us tickets because he had to go to his cousin's wedding. We watched Baltimore and Cleveland play. It was a long game, and we bought something to eat.

After the game, we walked out to the parking lot. The parking lot was in a big circle around the stadium. We walked around and around, but there were about 10,000 cars in the parking lot. We couldn't find our car! We forgot to check the section we parked in. After an hour, we stopped and sat down. We waited for an hour until the parking lot was almost empty. Then, we asked one of the security guards to drive us around. Finally, we found our car in section M5. From now on, I'm always going to check the section we park in. 🎧43

J Match the two parts of each sentence.

___d___ **1.** My friend was going to a wedding,

_____ **2.** We were hungry,

_____ **3.** We were very tired,

_____ **4.** We forgot to check our section,

_____ **5.** We couldn't find our car,

_____ **6.** There were thousands of cars in the lot,

a. so we couldn't find our car.

b. so we waited for most of them to leave.

c. so one of the security guards helped us.

d. so he gave us his tickets.

e. so we had something to eat.

f. so we stopped and rested.

A Write the past forms of the verbs in the box. Then, use the words to complete the story about important events in George's life. One word will be used twice.

graduate	_graduated_	be	_____	get	_____
find	_____	have	_____	fall	_____
save	_____	work	_____	buy	_____
meet	_____	quit	_____		

George _____graduated_____ from college in 2007 with a degree in biology.

He _____ a good job at a pharmaceutical company. Two years later, he

_____ Donna at a party. She _____ a kindergarten

teacher. They _____ in love and _____ married

in 2011. George and his wife _____ for the next three years, and they

_____ a lot of money. In 2014, they _____ a small

house. The next year, they _____ their first child—a little girl. Two years later,

they _____ another baby. Donna _____ her job and

now she stays home with the children.

B Answer these questions about George and Donna.

| Yes, he did. | Yes, she did. | Yes, they did. |
| No, he didn't. | No, she didn't. | No, they didn't. |

1. Did George graduate from college in 2006? _____ *No, he didn't.* _____

2. Did he major in biology? _____

3. Did George find a job at a hospital? _____

4. Did he meet Donna in 2009? _____

5. Did George and Donna meet at a party? _____

6. Did Donna teach high school? _____

7. Did they get married in 2011? _____

8. Did they buy a large house? _____

9. Did they have two children? _____

10. Did Donna quit her job? _____

C Choose the correct answer.

Alexander Graham Bell	Mary Shelley	Sally Ride
Amelia Earhart	Muhammad Ali	Thomas Edison
Frida Kahlo	~~Rosa Parks~~	Wolfgang Amadeus Mozart

1. Who fought for civil rights in the US? _____ *Rosa Parks did.* _____

2. Who composed famous operas? _____

3. Who invented the telephone? _____

4. Who flew solo across the Atlantic Ocean? _____

5. Who wrote *Frankenstein*? _____

6. Who painted many works of art? _____

7. Who won many boxing championships? _____

8. Who became the first American woman in space? _____

9. Who invented the electric light bulb? _____

D Complete the conversation with the sentences from the box.

> Did you find a good job?
>
> How much English did you know?
>
> What college did you attend?
>
> What did you major in?
>
> When did you come to this country?
>
> Where did you study English?
>
> ~~Where were you born?~~

A: _Where were you born?_

B: I was born in Haiti.

A: _____

B: I came here in 2008.

A: _____

B: I understood a little English.

A: _____

B: I went to a private language school for 18 months.

A: _____

B: I went to Fairfield University.

A: _____

B: I majored in engineering.

A: _____

B: Yes, I found a good job in a plastics company.

E Look at the pictures about Alex's life. Complete the questions on the next page.

2007   2009   2012

2014   2017

1. Where _was he born_ _____?   He was born in Hong Kong.

2. When _____?   He came to the US in 2007.

3. _____?   He moved to Boston in 2009.

4. _____?   He got a job at Bank of Boston.

5. _____?   He met Lena in 2014.

6. _____?   They got married in 2017.

F   Complete the questions about these important events.

1. What college _did she attend_ _____?

She attended Rice University.

2. What _____?

She majored in biology.

3. When _____?

She graduated in 2016.

4. Where _____?

They lived in New York.

5. When _____?

They moved in 2014.

6. Where _____?

They moved to Ohio.

7. When _____?

He retired last year.

8. How old _____?

He was 70 years old.

9. What _____?

The company gave him a watch.

LISTENING

G Listen and complete the questions with *Did* or *Were*. Then, answer the questions. 🎧 44

Yes, I was.	Yes, I did.
No, I wasn't.	No, I didn't.

1. _____Did_____ you sleep well last night? _____

2. _____ you do your homework? _____

3. _____ you at school yesterday? _____

4. _____ you sick last week? _____

5. _____ you take the bus to school today? _____

6. _____ you at a party last weekend? _____

7. _____ you call a friend last night? _____

8. _____ you drive to school yesterday? _____

9. _____ you home last night? _____

10. _____ you born in this country? _____

H Listen to these questions about the timeline. Circle the correct answers. 🎧 45

2010	Graduated from high school
2010–2012	Served in the army
2012	Failed police academy exam
2012–2014	Attended community college
2014	Passed police academy exam
2015	Graduated from the police academy
2017	Joined Greenwood police force

1. **a.** In 2010   **b.** In 2012   **c.** In 2014

2. **a.** In 2010   **b.** In Korea   **c.** Two years

3. **a.** Yes, he did.   **b.** No, he didn't.   **c.** In 2012

4. **a.** Once   **b.** Twice   **c.** In 2010

5. **a.** In 2012   **b.** One year   **c.** Two years

6. **a.** In 2014   **b.** In 2015   **c.** In 2017

7. **a.** In 2012   **b.** In 2015   **c.** In 2017

8. **a.** The police academy   **b.** In 2017   **c.** Greenwood

Pablo Picasso

Guernica, Picasso, 1937

Pablo Picasso is one of the most famous painters of the twentieth century. [1]He was born on October 25, 1881, in Málaga, Spain—the son of an art teacher. At an early age, Picasso showed great talent in drawing and painting. He was not interested in school, so he opened his own art studio when he was 16 years old.

When Picasso was a young man, he visited Paris, France. He fell in love with the city and moved there in 1904. Picasso painted the city, his neighbors, and everyday life in Paris. Picasso went through many periods as a painter. His Blue Period lasted from 1901 to 1904. Picasso used a lot of blue and gray during this time. The people in the paintings were long, thin, and unhappy. His Rose Period lasted from 1904 to 1906. Because he was happier at this time, his paintings were more colorful, and he used a lot of rose and pink in his art. After this, Picasso changed his style and painted in a more abstract and geometrical way.

One of Picasso's most famous paintings is *Guernica*. There was a civil war in Spain in 1936. Bombs fell on the city of Guernica and many men, women, and children died. Picasso was sad and angry. *Guernica* is a painting that protests war. The only colors in the painting are blacks, grays, and whites.

Picasso, the master of modern art, died in France on April 8, 1973. He was 91 years old. 🎧46

I Find the answers in the reading. <u>Underline</u> and number each answer.

1. Where was Picasso born?

2. Did he graduate from art school?

3. What city did he move to?

4. What did he paint?

5. How long was his Blue Period?

6. How did he feel during his Rose Period?

7. What is one of Picasso's most famous paintings?

8. Why did he paint it?

9. When did Picasso die?

A Write the comparative form of each adjective.

1. angry _____ *angrier* _____
2. athletic _____ *more athletic* _____
3. bad _____
4. beautiful _____
5. big _____
6. boring _____
7. careful _____
8. cheap _____
9. clean _____
10. comfortable _____
11. conservative _____
12. dirty _____
13. easy _____
14. energetic _____
15. expensive _____
16. famous _____
17. far _____
18. fast _____
19. friendly _____
20. good _____

21. handsome _____
22. happy _____
23. hardworking _____
24. heavy _____
25. intelligent _____
26. lazy _____
27. long _____
28. messy _____
29. modern _____
30. neat _____
31. noisy _____
32. old _____
33. organized _____
34. popular _____
35. pretty _____
36. punctual _____
37. quiet _____
38. small _____
39. tired _____
40. young _____

B Look at the pictures. Read the sentences and (circle) *True* or *False*.

1.	Lilia is lazier than Louisa.	(True)	False
2.	Louisa is more athletic than Lilia.	True	False
3.	Louisa's hair is longer than Lilia's hair.	True	False
4.	Lilia's hair is longer than Louisa's hair.	True	False
5.	Lilia is more active than Louisa.	True	False

Now, write two more sentences comparing yourself to one of your relatives.

6. _____

7. _____

C Compare the items. Use the adjectives in parentheses.

1. Chinese food / Italian food (delicious)

   *Italian food is more delicious than Chinese food.*_____

2. home-cooked food / restaurant food (fresh)

   _____

3. movies / TV (enjoyable)

   _____

4. shopping at the mall / watching TV (fun)

   _____

5. taking a test / working (stressful)

   _____

6. volleyball / soccer (exciting)

   _____

D Complete the sentences comparing the people in the pictures. Use the adjectives from the boxes.

Anne   Kathy

curly	neat	sloppy	~~straight~~	tall

1. Anne's hair is _____straighter than_____ Kathy's.

2. Kathy's hair is _____ Anne's.

3. Anne is _____ Kathy.

4. Kathy is _____ Anne.

5. Kathy is _____ Anne.

Steven   Mike

a good student	athletic	long	short

6. Steven's hair is _____ Mike's.

7. Mike's hair is _____ Steven's.

8. Mike is _____ Steven.

9. Steven is _____ Mike.

José   Olivia

focused	hardworking	sociable	talkative

10. José is _____ Olivia.

11. Olivia is _____ José.

12. Olivia is _____ José.

13. José is _____ Olivia.

E Look at the picture of the family. Write six sentences comparing the people in this family and their house to your family and your house. Use the adjectives in the box or other adjectives.

attractive	heavy	long hair	short		small	thin
big	large	old	short hair	tall		young

1. <u>My grandmother is shorter than Mary.</u>

2. <u>My grandparents are older than Mary and William.</u>

3. My family _____

4. My family _____

5. _____

6. _____

7. _____

8. _____

F Correct the <u>underlined</u> mistake in each sentence.

1. My cousin is ~~more~~ <u>stronger than</u> my brother.

2. Mr. Evans is <u>more talkative</u> ᵗʰᵃⁿ Mr. Smith.
   than

3. This job is <u>interestinger than</u> my last job.

4. Our secretary is <u>friendlier</u> your secretary.

5. This computer is <u>gooder than</u> that computer.

6. It's also <u>cheap than</u> that computer.

7. My house is <u>more far</u> from work than yours.

8. My sister is <u>short than</u> I am.

LISTENING

G Listen and (circle) the correct answer. 🎧47

1. Jack   (Julian)
2. Jack   Julian
3. Jack   Julian
4. Jack   Julian
5. Jack   Julian
6. Jack   Julian
7. Jack   Julian

Jack   Julian

H Listen and complete the conversation. 🎧48

Maggie: The superhero movie was great, wasn't it?

John: Are you kidding? The sci-fi movie we saw last week was _____ better _____

Maggie: The sci-fi movie had _____, but the superhero film was

_____.

John: You're right. The superhero movie was _____, but the sci-fi

film had _____ special effects.

Maggie: No way! The superhero movie had much _____ special effects.

I think the sci-fi movie was _____ the superhero film, though.

John: Yes, it was. So, you agree that the sci-fi movie was _____ the

superhero movie?

Maggie: You didn't hear anything I said!

I Listen to the conversation. (Circle) the adjectives that describe the mother's soup. 🎧49

  a. (saltier)   **c.** thinner   **e.** not spicy   **g.** tastier

  b. not salty   **d.** thicker   **f.** spicier   **h.** not tasty

Two Hotel Careers

The hotel clerk is one of the first people the guests see when they enter a hotel. The clerk works at the front desk and welcomes the guests. Hotel clerks must be polite and helpful. They have many responsibilities. They answer questions about the hotel and the area near the hotel. The hotel clerk works quickly, taking reservations and checking hotel bills. Hotel clerks also take care of problems. This is a difficult part of the job. Hotel clerks sometimes work with large groups of tourists. The clerks sometimes work long hours and overtime.

The schedules for hotel clerks depend on the hotel. They have flexible work schedules, but they often work weekends and evenings. In 2016, the average salary ranged from $17,470 to $31,850 or more. The salary can be higher according to the location, size, and type of hotel.

A good hotel chef can attract more hotel guests. Chefs supervise the work of the cooks and other kitchen workers. They order supplies and help plan and write menus. This is a stressful job. Chefs stand for many hours and lift heavy pots, often full of hot liquid. They work near hot ovens and grills. Burns are common injuries.

Most chefs have high school diplomas with some courses in business or management. Many study at special cooking institutes for one to three years. They also have many years of experience.

The schedules for hotel chefs can vary. Chefs can work early mornings, late evenings, holidays, and weekends. There are many opportunities for part-time work. In 2016, the average salary ranged from $23,630 to $76,280 or more. 🎧50

J   Read the statements comparing the two jobs and circle *True* or *False*.

1. A hotel clerk has less contact with hotel guests.	True	(False)
2. A hotel chef has more supervisory responsibilities.	True	False
3. Working with people is an important part of both jobs.	True	False
4. Both jobs have varying schedules.	True	False
5. A hotel chef makes more decisions than a desk clerk.	True	False
6. A hotel chef needs to be stronger than a desk clerk.	True	False
7. A hotel clerk has a safer job than a hotel chef.	True	False
8. A hotel clerk's starting salary is higher than a chef's.	True	False

A Write a sentence about each picture. Use the future with *be going to.*

1. _____He is going to take a shower._____   5. _____

2. _____   6. _____

3. _____   7. _____

4. _____   8. _____

B Complete the two sentences about each picture. Use the future with *be going to*. One sentence for each picture is affirmative and one sentence is negative.

1. She _____is not going to cook_____ (cook) tonight.

2. She _____is going to order_____ (order) Chinese food.

3. They _____ (stay) home tonight.

4. They _____ (go) to the movies.

5. He _____ (get up) early.

6. He _____ (stay) in bed until 11:00.

7. He _____ (work) anymore.

8. He _____ (retire).

9. It's raining, so she _____ (run) in the park.

10. She _____ (work out) at the gym.

11. He _____ (work) from 10:30 to 10:45.

12. He _____ (take) a fifteen-minute break.

C Look at each object. What are you going to do?

1. I _am going to cut the grass._ _____

2. I _____

3. I _____

4. I _____

5. I _____

D Answer the questions about Erica's plans for next week.

Sunday	Monday	Tuesday	Wednesday	Thursday	Friday	Saturday
Work 7:00–3:00	Work 7:00–3:00	Work 7:00–3:00	Beach	Work 7:00–3:00	Work 7:00–3:00	Work 7:00–3:00
Buy present for baby shower	Gym 4:00	School 7:00–9:00	Bank – apply for car loan	School 7:00–9:00	Gym 4:00	Baby shower 3:00
	Study for test	Test			Eat out with Rosa	

1. How many days is Erica going to work next week?

   She is going to work six days next week.

2. What is Erica going to do after work on Sunday?

   _____

3. What days is Erica going to go to the gym?

   _____

4. When is Erica going to take a test?

   _____

5. When is she going to study for the test?

   _____

6. Where is Erica going to go on her day off from work?

   _____

7. What is Erica going to do at the bank?

   _____

8. Who is Erica going to see on Friday night?

   _____

9. What time is the baby shower going to start?

   _____

10. What time is Erica going to arrive at the baby shower?

    _____

E Complete the predictions about each person's future. Use *will* and a verb from the box.

buy	go	~~stop~~
celebrate	graduate	study
find	have	visit
get married	move	volunteer

1. He _____will stop_____ working tomorrow.

2. He _____ to Florida.

3. He _____ for the Red Cross.

4. He _____ his grandchildren every week.

5. She _____ from high school next year.

6. She _____ to college next year.

7. She _____ business.

8. She _____ a good job.

9. They _____ next summer.

10. They _____ a short honeymoon.

11. They _____ a house.

12. They _____ their anniversary every year.

F Listen to each conversation. Circle *True* or *False*. 🎧51

Conversation 1

1. Paula isn't going to go to work today.   (True)   False

2. Paula is going to drive to the hospital.   True   False

3. Paula broke her arm.   True   False

4. Jim is going to ask Maria to work overtime.   True   False

Conversation 2

5. Both of these men are working.   True   False

6. Bob is going to move to Virginia.   True   False

7. Bob is going to open a restaurant.   True   False

8. His wife is going to be a waitress.   True   False

G Listen to each sentence. Write the verb you hear. Listen carefully. The verbs are in different forms. 🎧52

1. Tony _____*stopped*_____ at the red light.

2. Gerry _____ the back of Tony's car.

3. Tony _____ the police.

4. Gerry _____ a ticket.

5. Gerry's insurance _____ for the damages.

6. Diana _____ in her daughter's bedroom.

7. Her daughter _____ late this morning.

8. She _____ time to clean her room.

9. Diana _____ clean the room.

10. Her daughter _____ her room when she gets home.

H Listen to each question. Write the correct object pronoun: *me, you, him, her, it,* or *them.* 🎧53

1. I am going to call _____him_____ tonight.

2. I am going to visit _____ tomorrow.

3. I am going to see _____ on Friday.

4. I am going to wash _____ this afternoon.

5. I am going to read _____ soon.

6. I am going to call _____ tonight.

7. I am going to drive _____ at 8:00.

8. She is going to help _____ after dinner.

9. I am going to marry _____ in June.

10. I am going to clean _____ this weekend.

READING Personal Narrative

My Plan

I am a single mother with a six-year-old daughter. For five years, I worked in a car factory, installing car doors. Last week, our factory closed. Thousands of people in my city are looking for jobs. Everyone is upset, but I'm okay. I have a plan.

First, I'm going to apply for unemployment. I'm going to receive about $800 a month. Next, I'm going to move to Connecticut. My sister lives there, and I'm going to stay with her for a few months. I'm going to find a job as a locksmith. A locksmith installs locks and opens house and car doors when a person loses the key. A locksmith also installs security systems in homes, stores, and offices. This job is perfect for me. I'm good with my hands, and I like mechanical things. I can learn on the job. Also, I think that this is a good job for a parent because the schedule is flexible. I can change it if I need to. 🎧54

I Answer the questions.

1. What does a locksmith do?

   a. A locksmith installs locks. _____

   b. _____

   c. _____

2. Why is this a good job for this woman?

   a. _____

   b. _____

   c. _____

VACATIONS

A Look at the pictures. Everyone is thinking about vacation plans. Read and answer the questions.

Yes, she is.	Yes, he is.	Yes, they are.
No, she isn't.	No, he isn't.	No, they aren't.

1. Are they going to catch some fish next month?

   _____ Yes, they are. _____

2. Are they going to go swimming in a lake?

   _____

3. Is he going to go to a park next summer?

   _____

4. Is he going to relax on the beach?

   _____

5. Are they going to visit a museum next week?

   _____

6. Are they going to see many kinds of fish?

   _____

7. Is Mei-Lin going to visit an art museum on her vacation?

   _____

8. Is she going to go with her class?

   _____

9. Is George going to see a soccer game next month?

   _____

10. Is he going to have a good time?

   _____

B Complete the questions and answers about next summer. Use *be* + *going to* and the verbs in parentheses.

Am	I		
Are	you we they	**going to**	visit a museum? swim in a lake? go to a carnival?
Is	she he		

1. ____Are____ tourists _____*going to visit*_____ (visit) a national park this weekend?

   _____*Yes, they are.*_____

2. _____ Hank and Vanessa _____ (rent) a house in July?

   _____

3. _____ they _____ (stay) in a hotel?

   _____

4. _____ Linda _____ (take) a tour of New York City?

   _____

5. _____ she _____ (go) with her boyfriend?

   _____

6. _____ Mr. Carter _____ (take) his family to a baseball park?

   _____

7. _____ he _____ (play) baseball?

   _____

8. _____ Ginger _____ (spend) time at the beach this weekend?

   _____

9. _____ she _____ (go) surfing?

   _____

C Look at the picture. Complete the questions about the Rose family's vacation. Use the words in parentheses.

What	**am**	I		
Where		you		
When	**are**	we		
Who		they	**going to**	visit?
How	**is**	he		
How long		she		
Who	**is**	—		

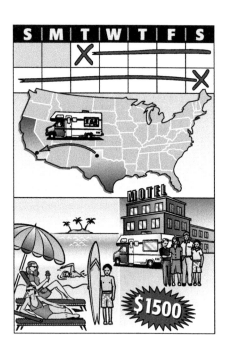

1. _____Is the Rose family going to go_____ on vacation?

    (the Rose family / go)

    Yes, they are.

2. How _____?

    (they / travel)

    By RV.

3. How long _____?

    (they / stay)

    For twelve days.

4. Where _____?

    (they / stay)

    In a motel near the beach.

5. What _____?

    (their son Jason / do)

    He's going to go surfing.

6. Who _____?

    (go / swimming)

    Their son Mike is.

7. _____ a good time?

    (everyone / have)

    Yes, they are.

8. Where _____ this vacation?

    (they / spend)

    In California.

D Look at the information in the chart below. Write the questions and answers. Use the future with *be + going to.*

Who	Laura Home: Rome	The Tanaka family Home: Tokyo
Where / next summer	Barcelona, Spain	Maui, Hawaii
What	go sightseeing study Spanish	go surfing and swimming visit their grandparents
How long	four weeks	ten days
How	by train	fly

1. Who is from Rome _____?

   Laura is. _____

2. Where is she going to go next summer _____?

   _____

3. What _____?

   _____

4. How long _____?

   _____

5. How _____?

   _____

6. Who _____?

   The Tanaka family is. _____

7. Where _____?

   _____

8. What _____?

   _____

9. How long _____?

   _____

10. How _____?

   _____

LISTENING

E Listen and circle the correct answer. 🎧 55

1. **a.** Yes, they do. **b.** Yes, they are. **c.** Yes, there are.

2. **a.** No, it doesn't. **b.** No, there isn't. **c.** Yes, it is.

3. **a.** No, he doesn't. **b.** No, he isn't. **c.** No, he didn't.

4. **a.** I'm a student. **b.** I'm studying. **c.** I'm going to study.

5. **a.** He's washing the car. **b.** He's going to wash the car. **c.** He washes his car every week.

6. **a.** She's taking a test. **b.** She took a test. **c.** She takes tests.

7. **a.** I'm going to Canada. **b.** I went to Canada. **c.** I'm in Canada.

8. **a.** I stayed for two weeks. **b.** I stay for two weeks. **c.** I'm going to stay for two weeks.

9. **a.** Yes, I am. **b.** Yes, I do. **c.** Yes, I did.

10. **a.** They're going to arrive next weekend. **b.** They arrived yesterday. **c.** They arrive at 4:00 every day.

F Listen and write the questions. Then, answer them. 🎧 56

1. _What are you going to do tonight?_ _____

   Answer: _____

2. _____

   Answer: _____

3. _____

   Answer: _____

4. _____

   Answer: _____

5. _____

   Answer: _____

6. _____

   Answer: _____

7. _____

Answer: _____

8. _____

Answer: _____

A Visit to Washington, D.C.

Every year, thousands of visitors go to Washington, D.C., the capital of the United States. It is a district, or area, ¹between the states of Virginia and Maryland. It is a popular city for tourists because of its government, history, and museums. In the spring, tourists enjoy the National Cherry Blossom Festival to celebrate D.C.'s beautiful cherry trees, a gift from Japan.

The National Mall is a two-and-a-half-mile long area. It is between the Potomac River and the United States Capitol. The US Capitol is at one end. The Lincoln Memorial is at the opposite end. The Smithsonian Institution is a group of museums, galleries, and the National Zoo. There are no admission fees because they are national museums. The National Air and Space Museum and the National Museum of African American History and Culture are two examples. There is something for everyone at the Smithsonian.

Tourists like to visit the various monuments and memorials in the National Mall area. There are four places that honor former presidents. The Washington Monument honors the first president, George Washington. The Thomas Jefferson Memorial honors the third president. The Lincoln Memorial honors Abraham Lincoln, the sixteenth president. There is also a monument to Franklin D. Roosevelt. He was the thirty-second president. 🔊 57

G Read the questions. Then, number and underline the answers in the reading.

1. Where is Washington, D.C.?

2. Why is Washington, D.C. popular with tourists?

3. When is the National Cherry Blossom Festival?

4. What country gave Washington, D.C. the cherry trees?

5. Where is the National Mall?

6. What is the Smithsonian Institution?

7. How many monuments honor former presidents?

8. Who was the third president of the United States?

SPELLING RULES

Plural Nouns

1. For most nouns, add an -s.
   boy – boys   store – stores   student – students

2. If a noun ends with a consonant and a *y*, change the *y* to *i*, and add -es.
   city – cities   dictionary – dictionaries   baby – babies

3. If a noun ends with *sh, ch, x*, or *z*, add -es.
   dish – dishes   watch – watches   box – boxes

Present Continuous Verbs

1. For most verbs, add -*ing*.
   walk – walking   play – playing   eat – eating

2. If a verb ends in *e*, drop the *e* and add -*ing*.
   write – writing   come – coming   drive – driving

3. If a verb ends in a consonant + vowel + consonant, double the final consonant and add -*ing*.
   sit – sitting   run – running   put – putting

Present: Third Person

1. For most verbs, add -*s*.
   make – makes   call – calls   sleep – sleeps

2. If a verb ends with a consonant and a *y*, change the *y* to *i*, and add -es.
   try – tries   cry – cries   apply – applies

3. If a verb ends with *sh, ch, x*, or *z*, add -es.
   wash – washes   watch – watches   fix – fixes

4. These verbs are irregular in the third person.
   have – has   do – does

Past Verbs

1. For most verbs, add *-d* or *-ed*.
   save – saved   rent – rented

2. If a verb ends in a consonant + *y*, change the *y* to *i* and add *-ed*.
   try – tried   study – studied

3. If a verb ends in a consonant + vowel + consonant, double the final consonant and add *-ed*.
   stop – stopped   rob – robbed

4. If a verb ends in *w*, *x*, or *y*, do not double the consonant. Add *-ed*.
   play – played   relax – relaxed   snow – snowed

Comparative Adjectives: *-er*

1. For most adjectives, add *-r* or *-er*.
   cold – colder   short – shorter   tall – taller

2. If a one-syllable adjective ends in a consonant + vowel + consonant, double the final consonant and add *-er*.
   big – bigger   thin – thinner   sad – sadder

3. If an adjective ends in a consonant + *y*, change the *y* to *i* and add *-er*.
   happy – happier   heavy – heavier   friendly – friendlier

IRREGULAR PAST VERBS

Present	Past	Present	Past	Present	Past	Present	Past
be	was, were	fall	fell	lose	lost	speak	spoke
begin	began	feel	felt	make	made	spend	spent
break	broke	find	found	meet	met	stand	stood
bring	brought	fly	flew	pay	paid	take	took
build	built	forget	forgot	put	put	teach	taught
buy	bought	get	got	read	read	tell	told
come	came	give	gave	run	ran	think	thought
cost	cost	go	went	say	said	understand	understood
cut	cut	grow	grew	see	saw	wake	woke
do	did	have	had	send	sent	wear	wore
drink	drank	hear	heard	sing	sang	win	won
drive	drove	know	knew	sit	sat	write	wrote
eat	ate	leave	left	sleep	slept		

CREDITS